T0085546

Herbert Howells
Three Psalm Preludes for Organ

Set one

Cover drawing by BRENDA MOORE, reproduced by permission of
the Royal College of Music.

Order No: NOV 590353

NOVELLO PUBLISHING LIMITED

To Sir Walter Parratt.

PSALM - PRELUDE

I.

Ps. 34. v. 6.

Herbert Howells, Op. 32, No 1.

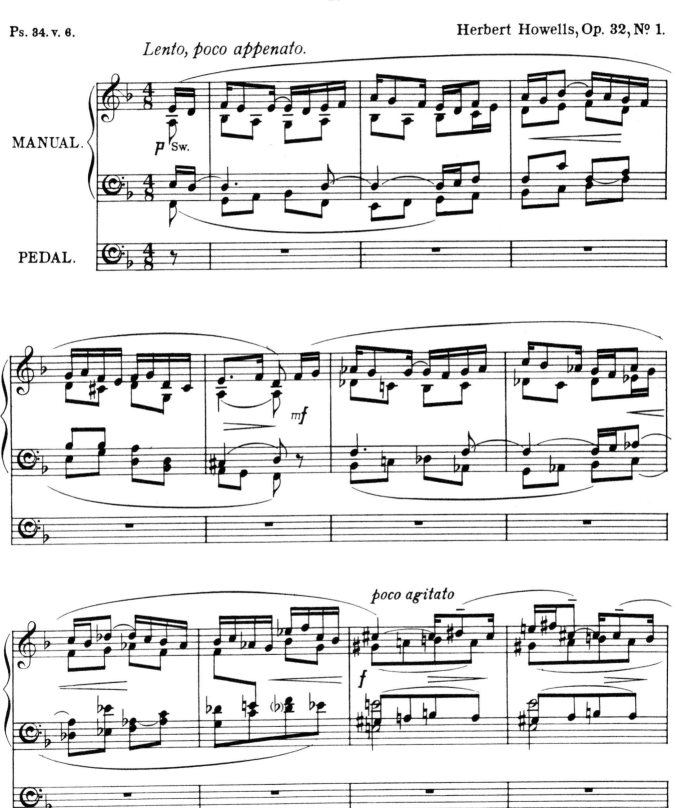

4

8

PSALM - PRELUDE
II.

Ps. 37. v. 11.

Herbert Howells, Op. 32, № 2.

Non troppo lento, ma sempre espressivo.

MANUAL.

PEDAL.

12

(H.H. 1916)

To Sydney Shimmin.

PSALM-PRELUDE
III.

Ps. 23. v. 4.

Herbert Howells, Op. 32. Nº 3.

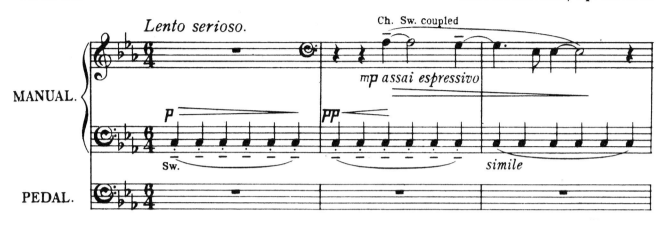

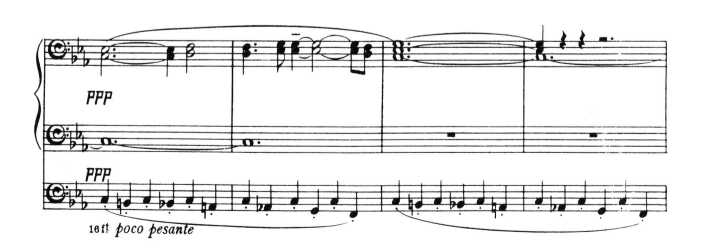

* Throughout this page the rhythm must not be rigid.

Più mosso, e poco agitato

ancora più mosso e più agitato

18

(H. H. 1915)

ORGAN ALBUMS

ed Allan Wicks
CANTERBURY ORGAN ALBUM

ed John Sanders
GLOUCESTER ORGAN ALBUM

ed Francis Jackson
YORK ORGAN ALBUM

The first three collections in a unique series featuring music by the organists of England's great cathedrals. Each volume also contains the specification of the cathedral organ together with biographical details and pictures of the composers.

ELGAR ORGAN ALBUM Book 1
Cantique
Adagio from the Cello Concerto
Carillon
Solemn Prelude *In memoriam* from 'For the Fallen'
Imperial March

ELGAR ORGAN ALBUM Book 2
Nimrod from 'Enigma Variations'
Triumphal March from 'Caractacus'
Funeral March from 'Grania and Diarmid'
Prelude and Angel's Farewell from 'The Dream of Gerontius'

PARRY ORGAN ALBUM Book 1
Fantasia and Fugue in G
Chorale Fantasia on 'The Old Hundredth'
Elegy for April 7, 1913

PARRY ORGAN ALBUM Book 2
Toccata and Fugue (The Wanderer)
Chorale Fantasia on 'O God Our Help'
Chorale Fantasia on An Old English Tune

ed Robert Gower
ORGAN MUSIC OF JOHN IRELAND
Sursum Corda
Alla Marcia
Elegiac Romance
Intrada
Villanella
Menuetto
The Holy Boy
Meditation
Capriccio